Welcome to Fairies & Mermaids Coloring Book

By: AH64Designs

Inside you will find 20 full pages of adorable fantasy inspired Fairies & Mermaids coloring art.

Never stop having fun!

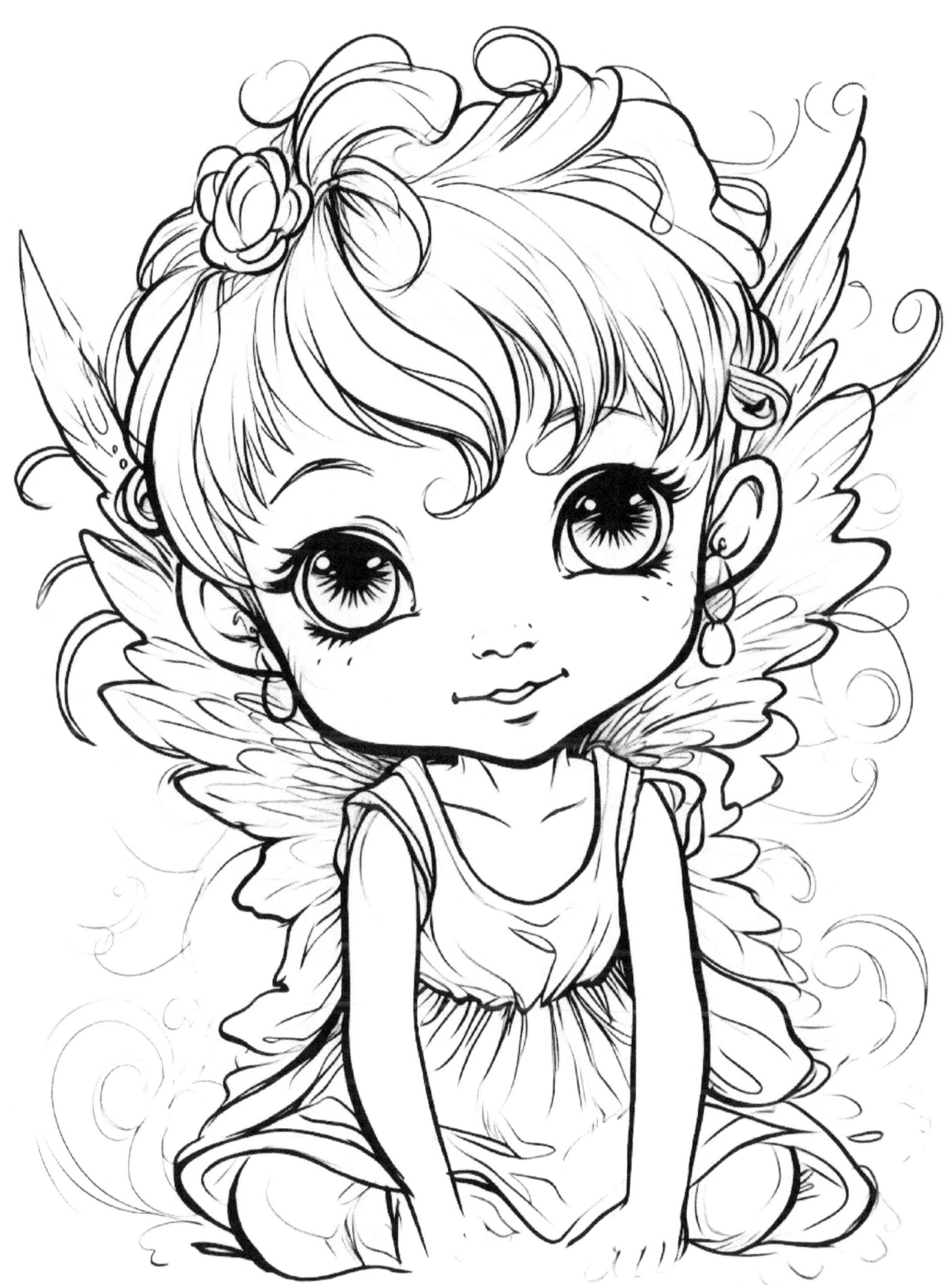

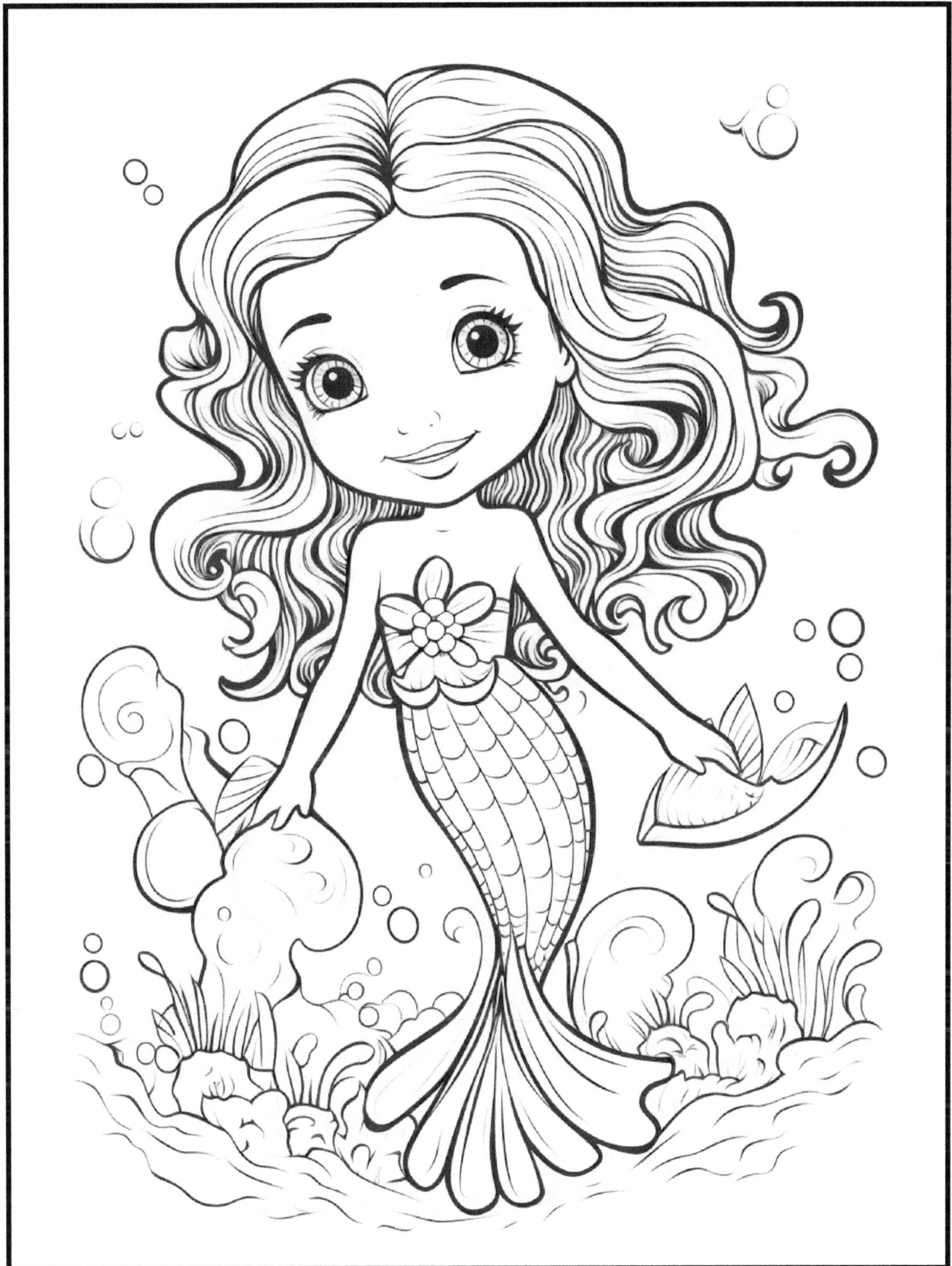

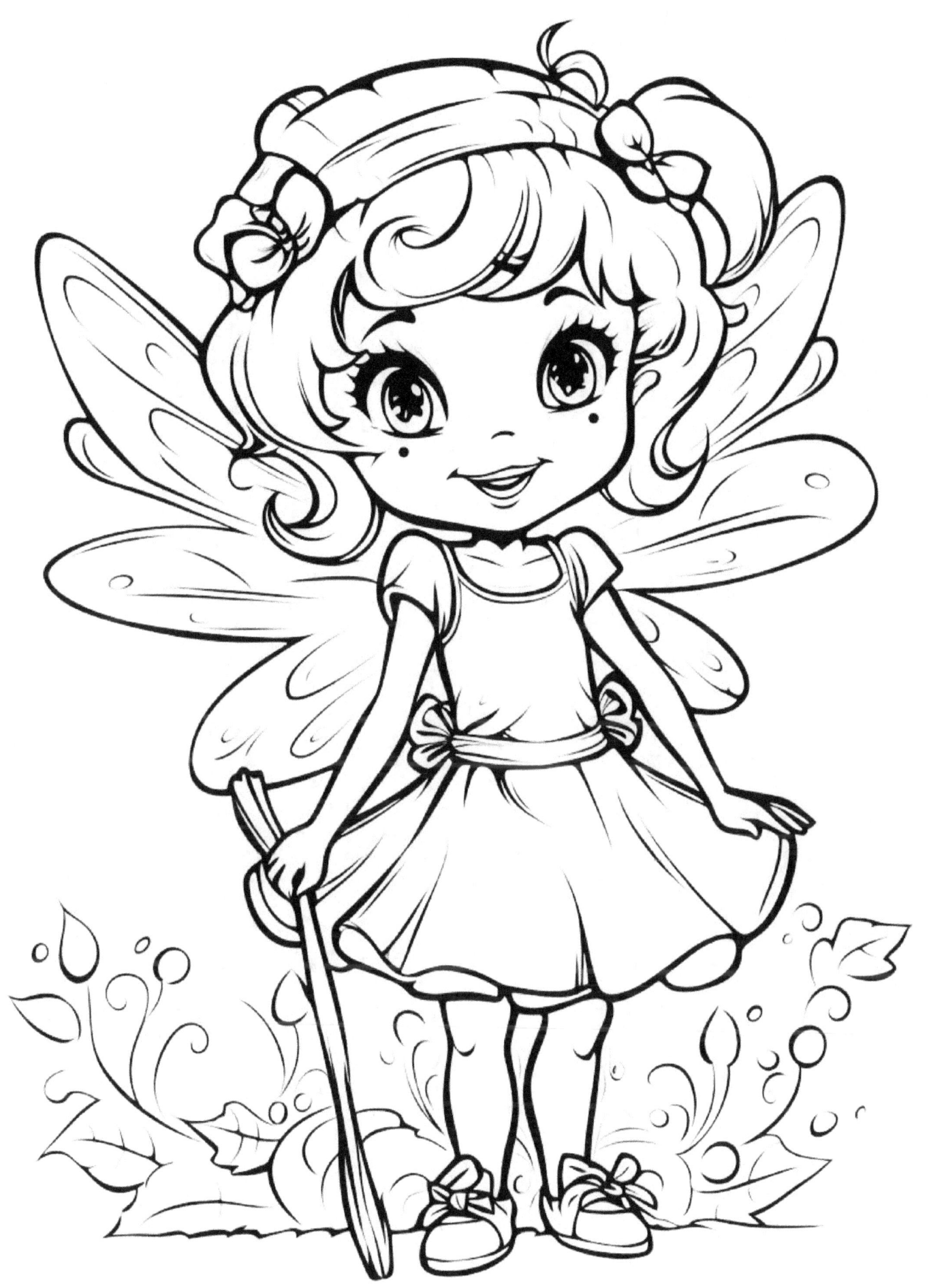

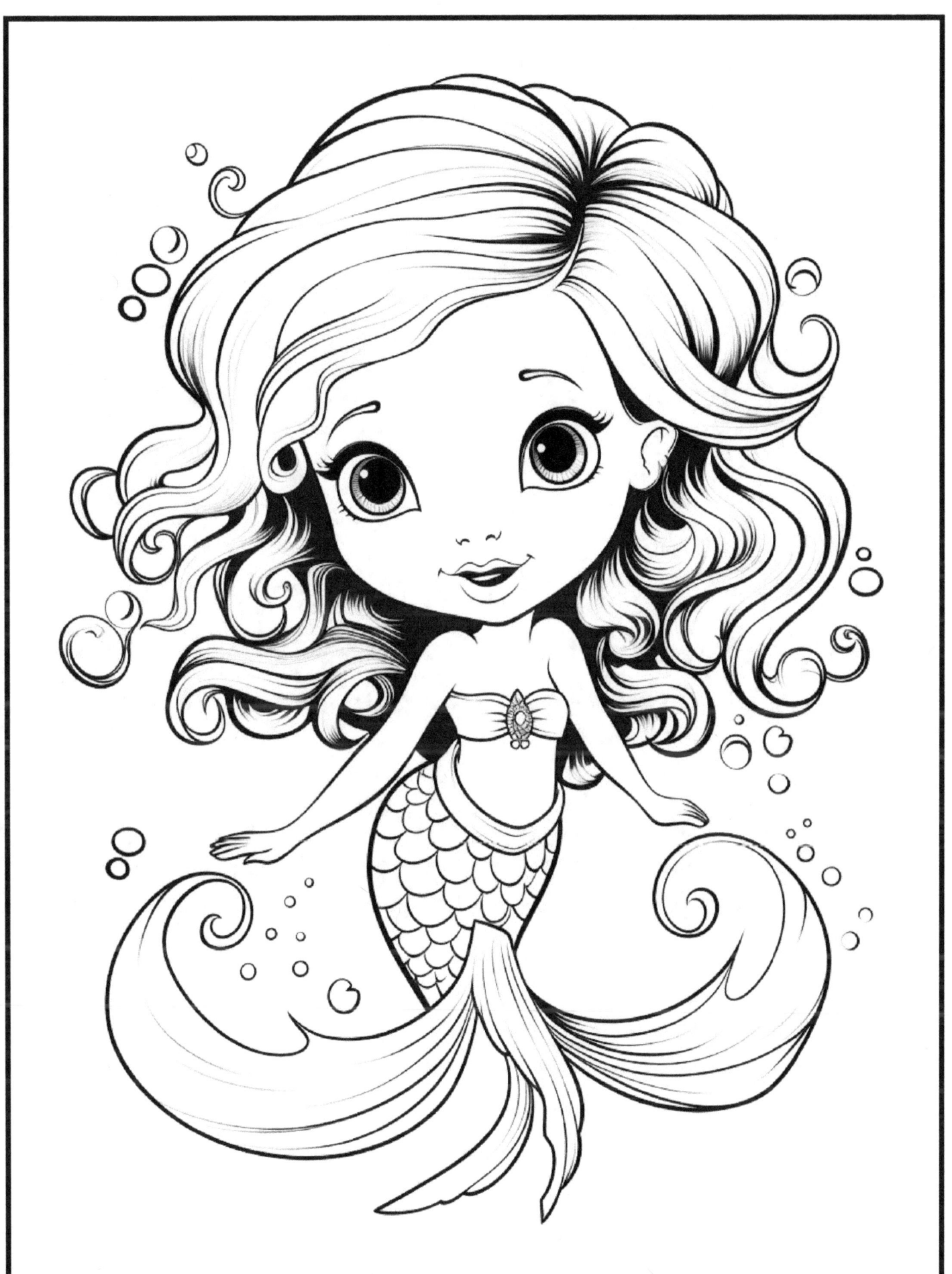

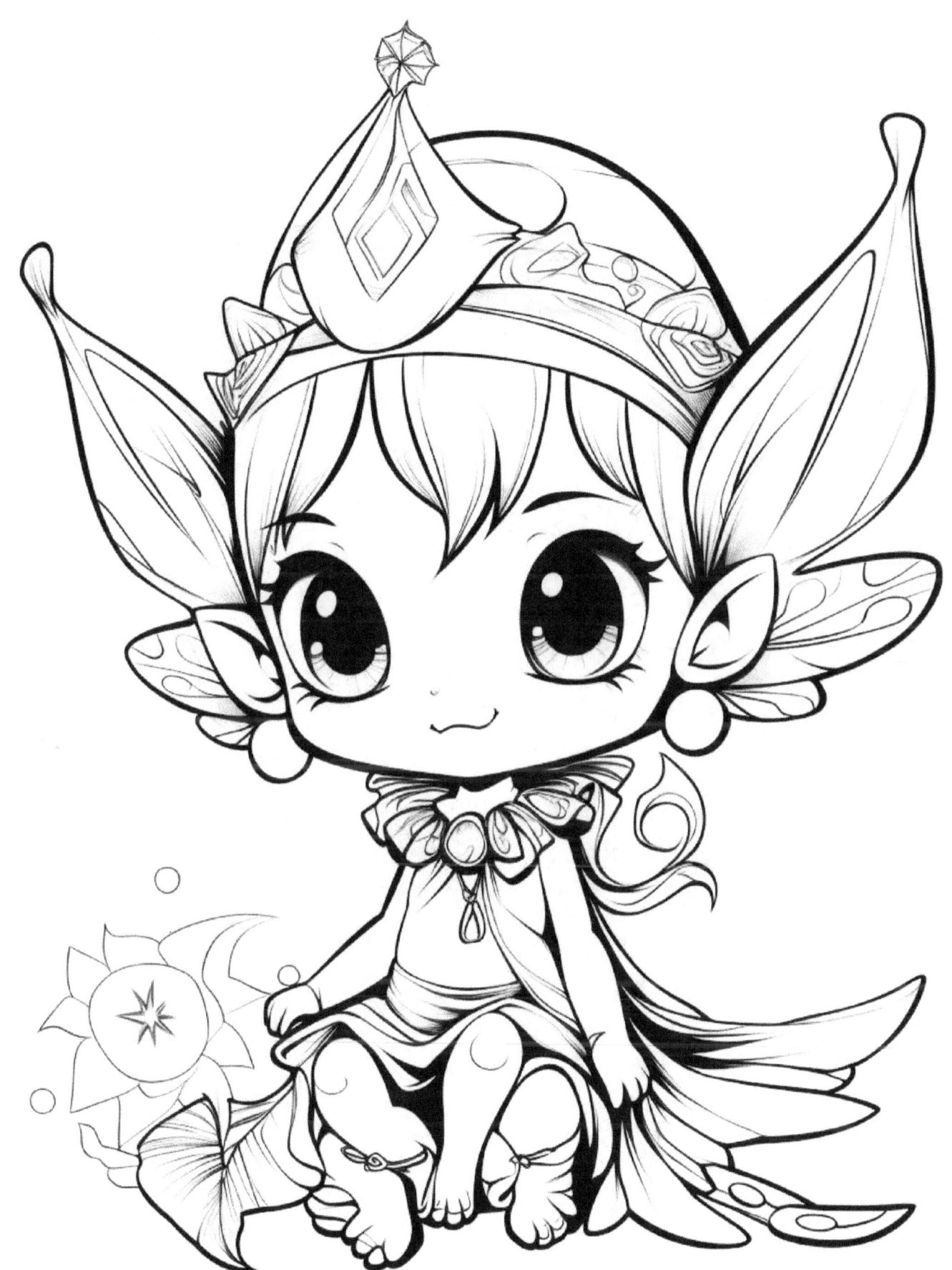

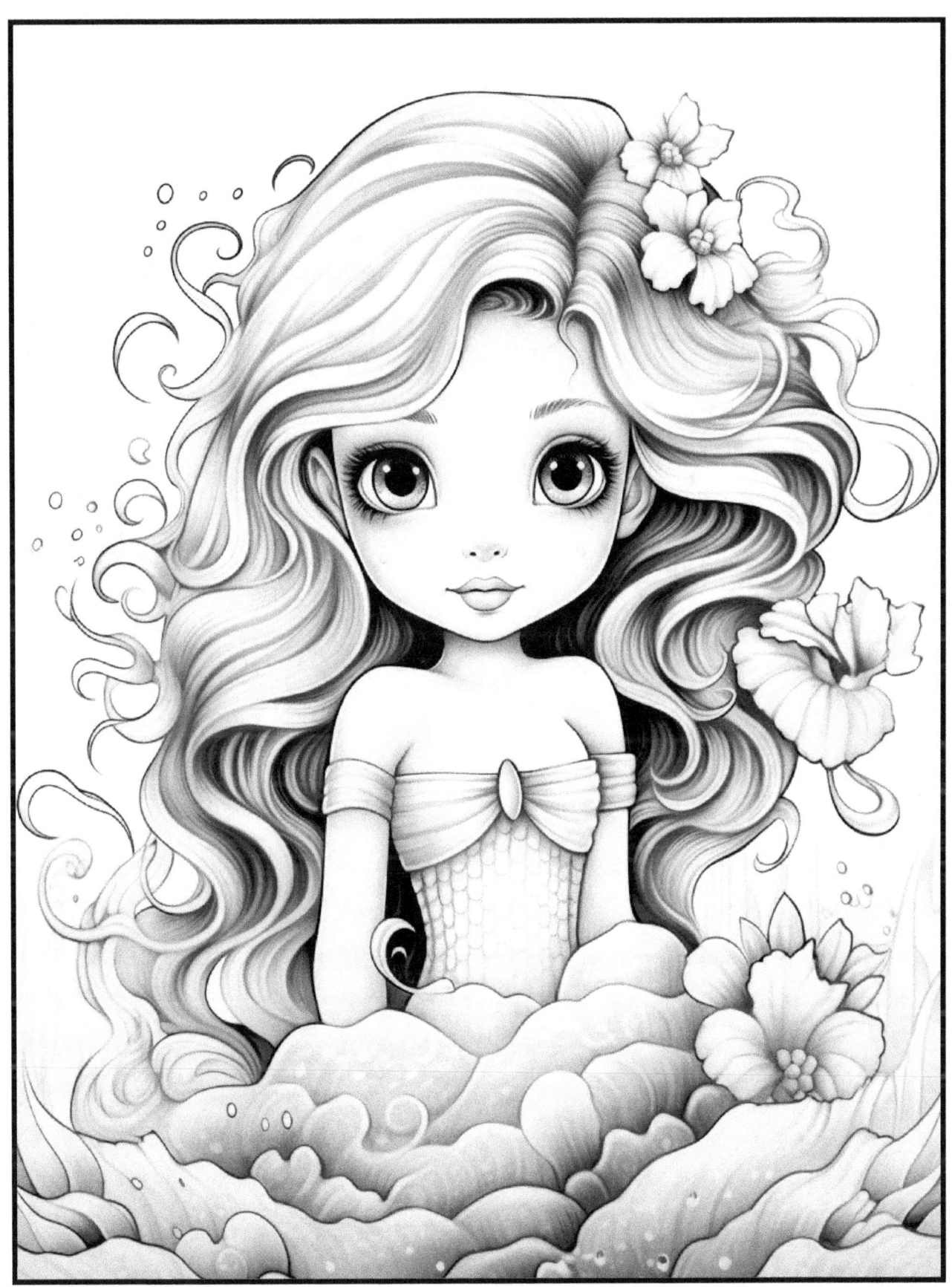

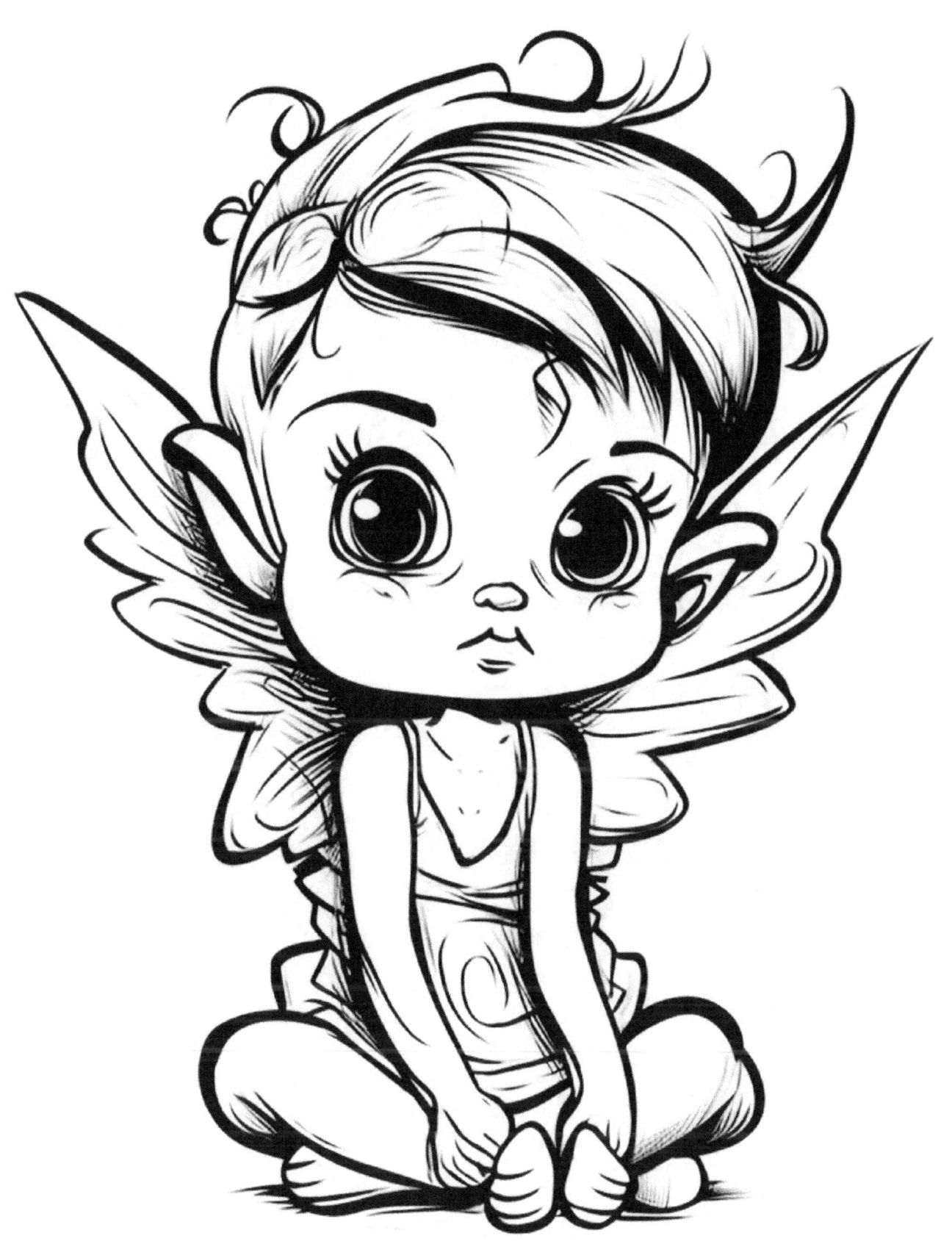

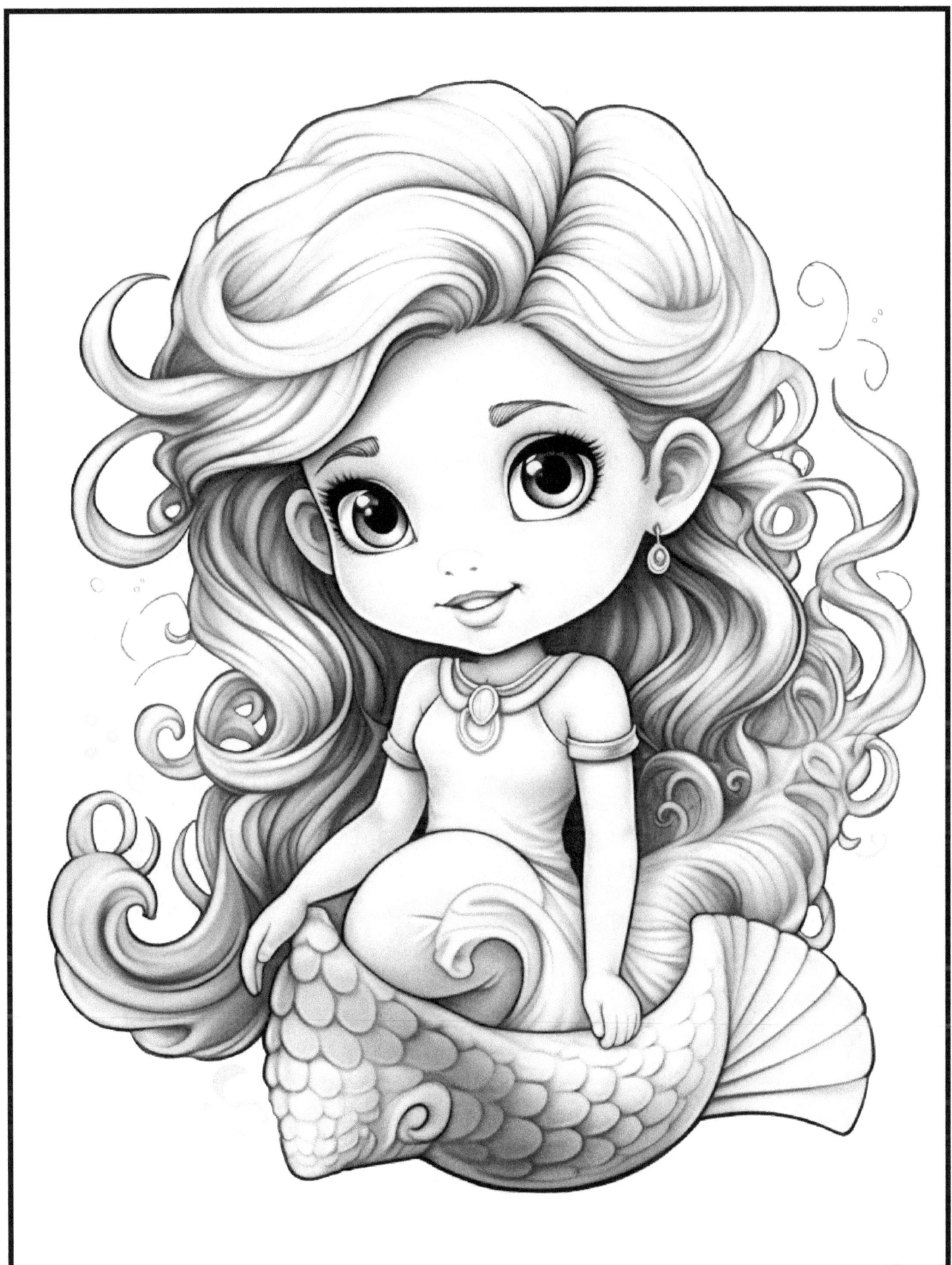

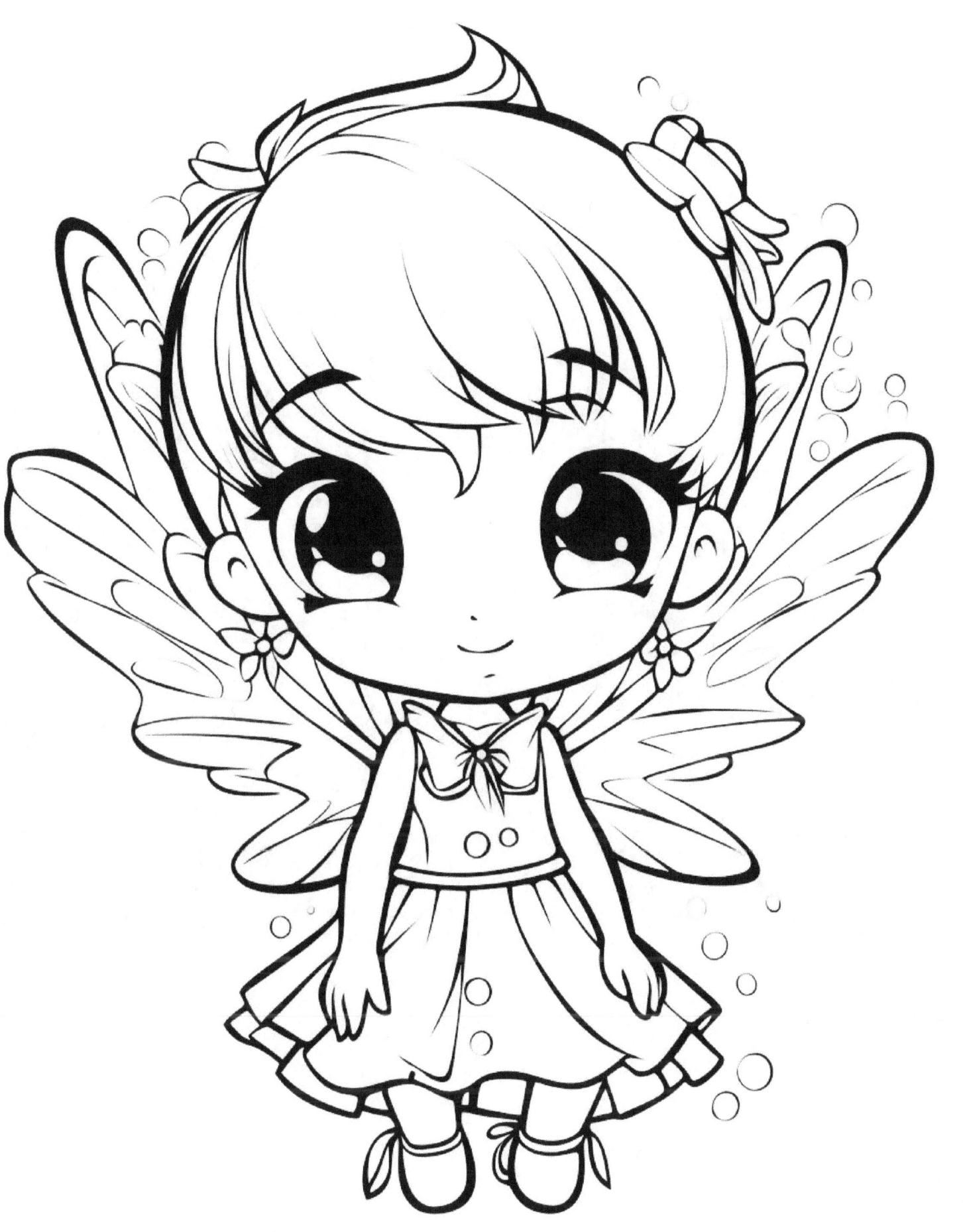

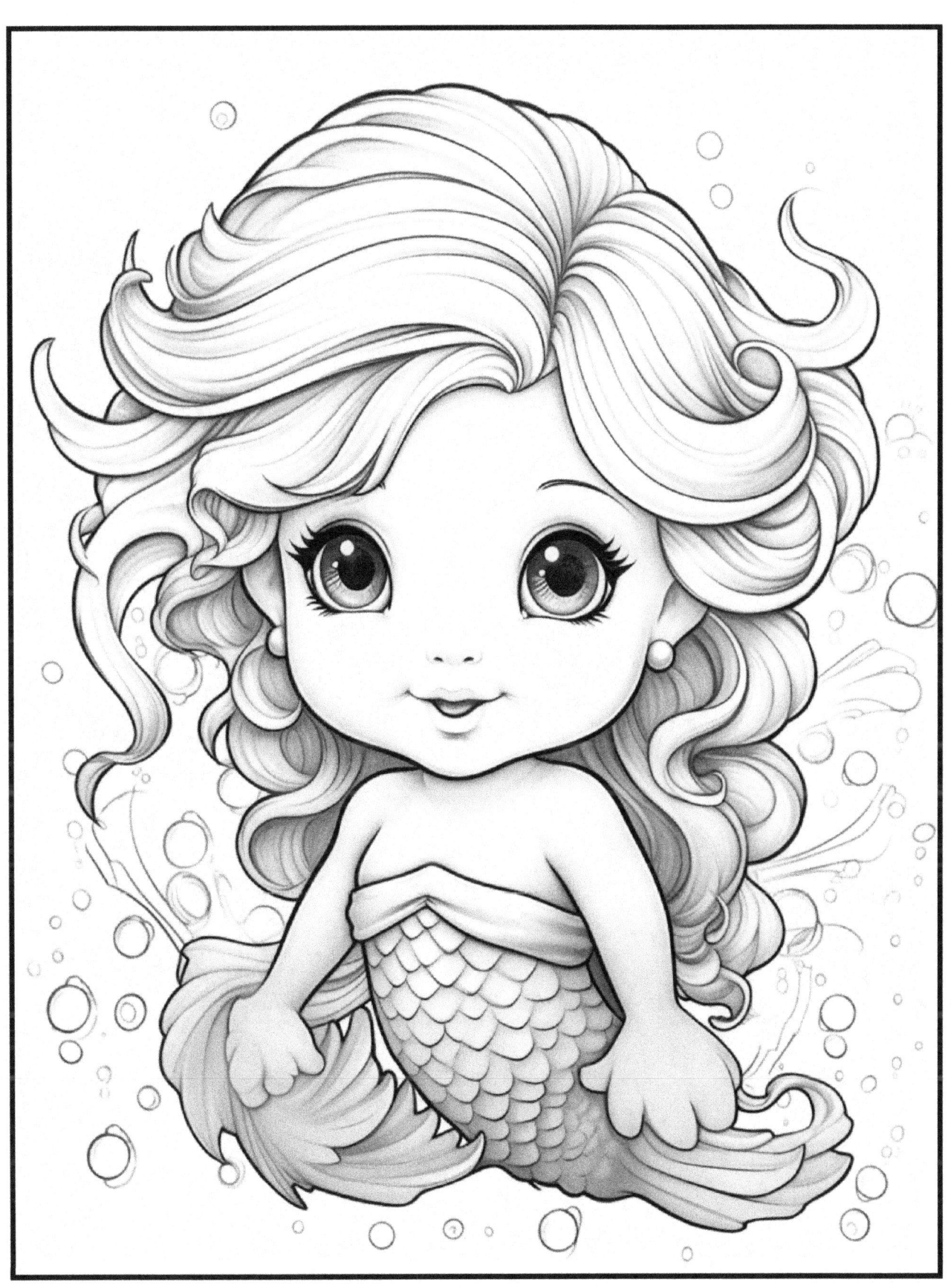

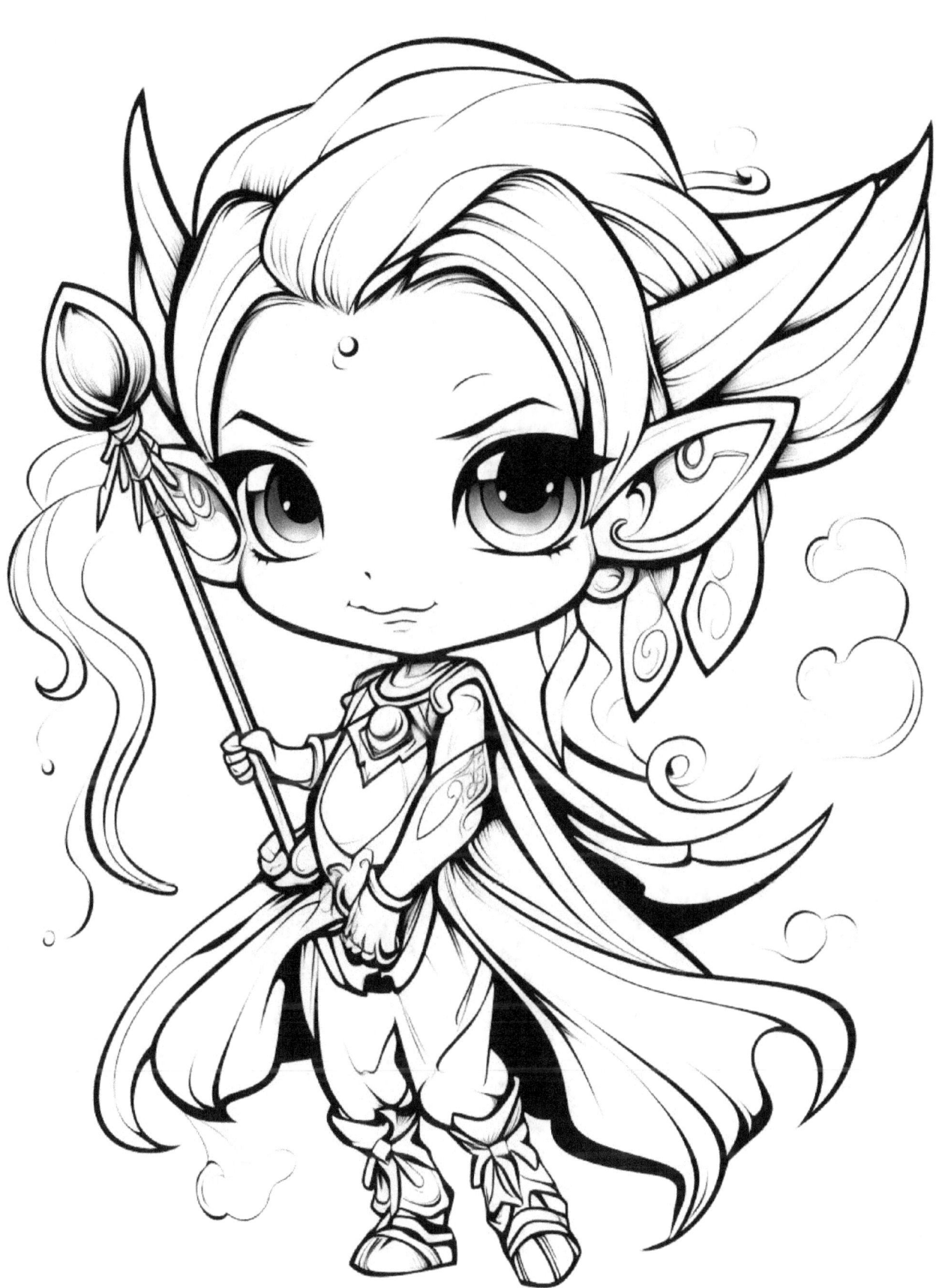

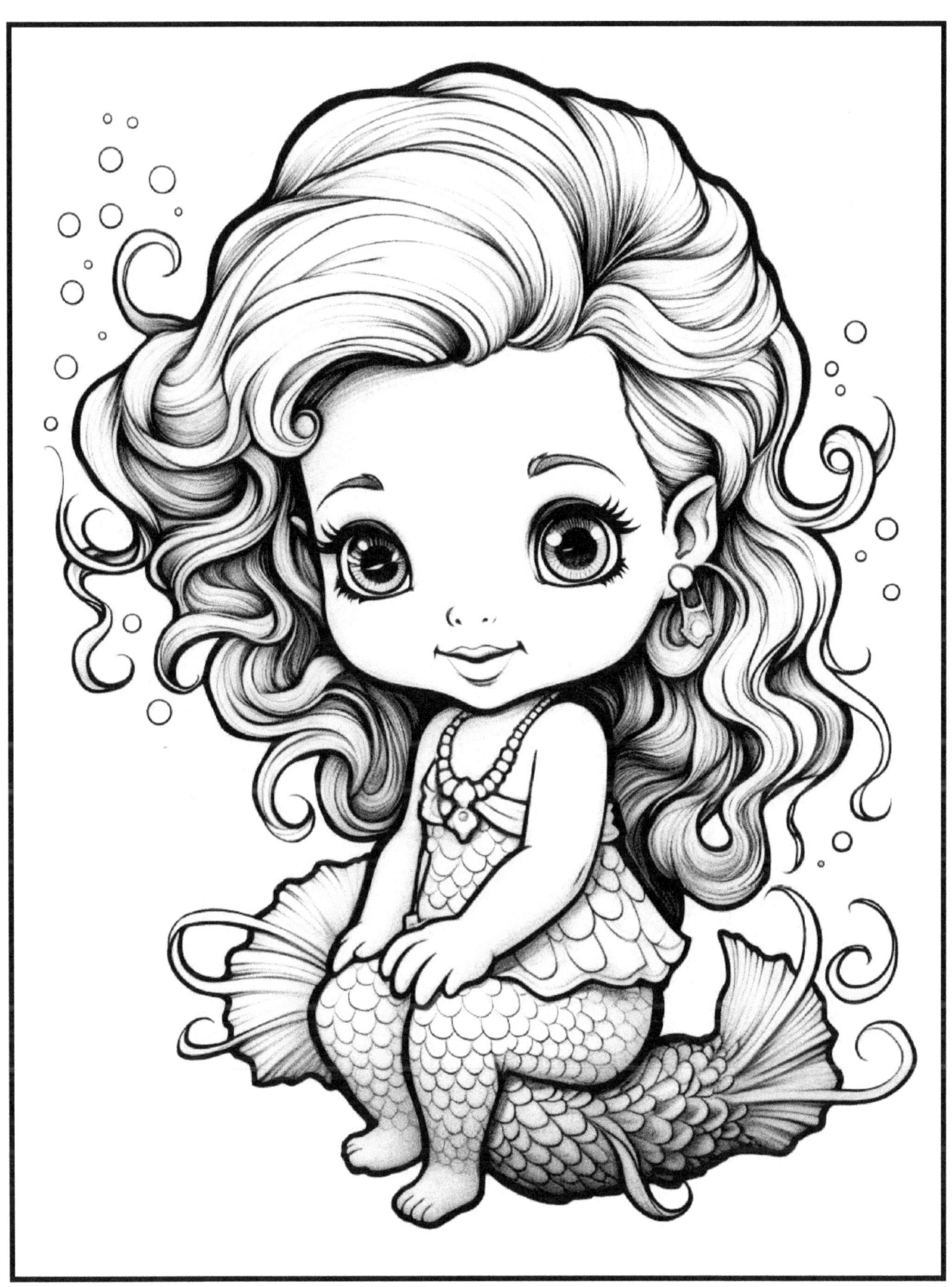

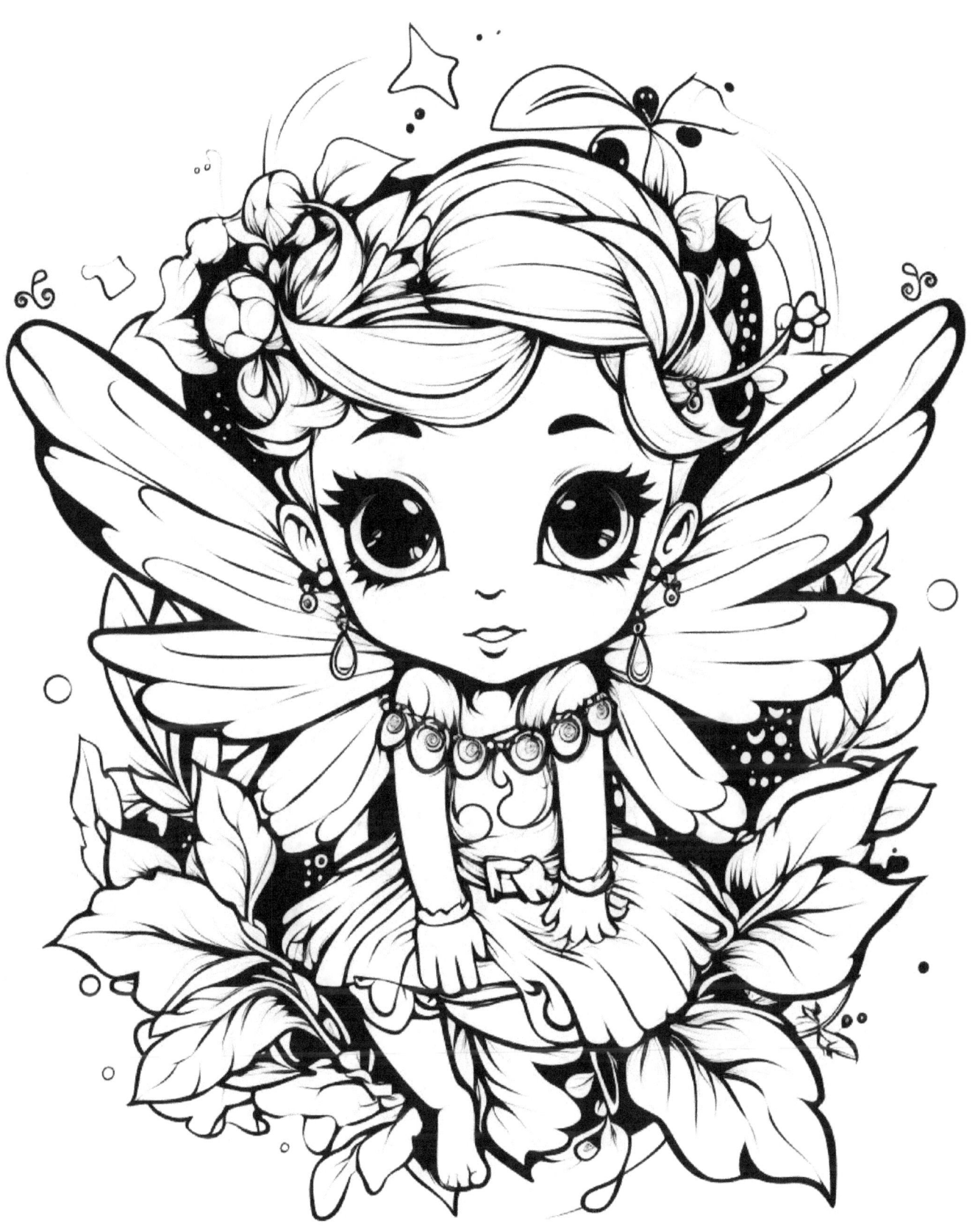

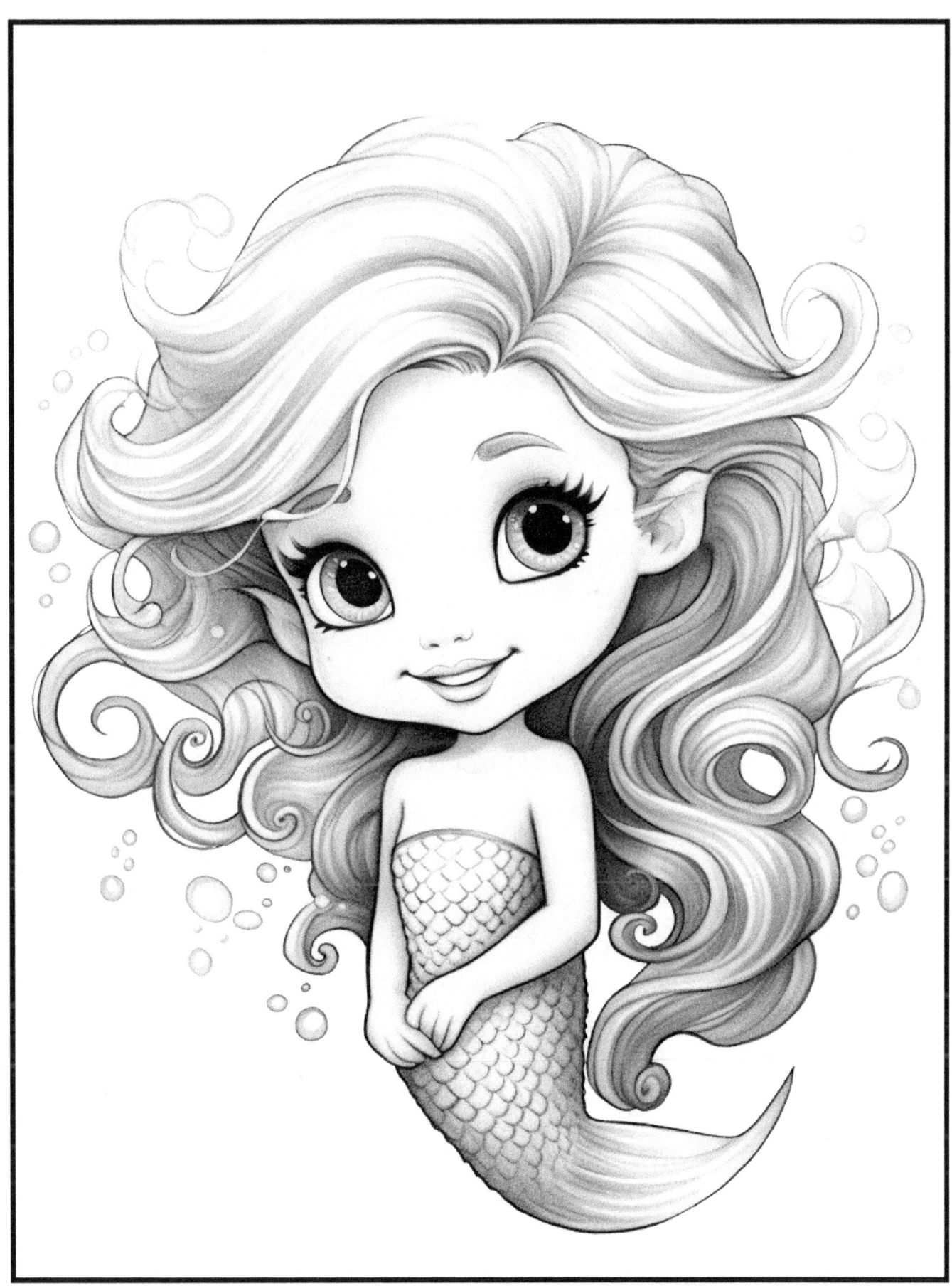

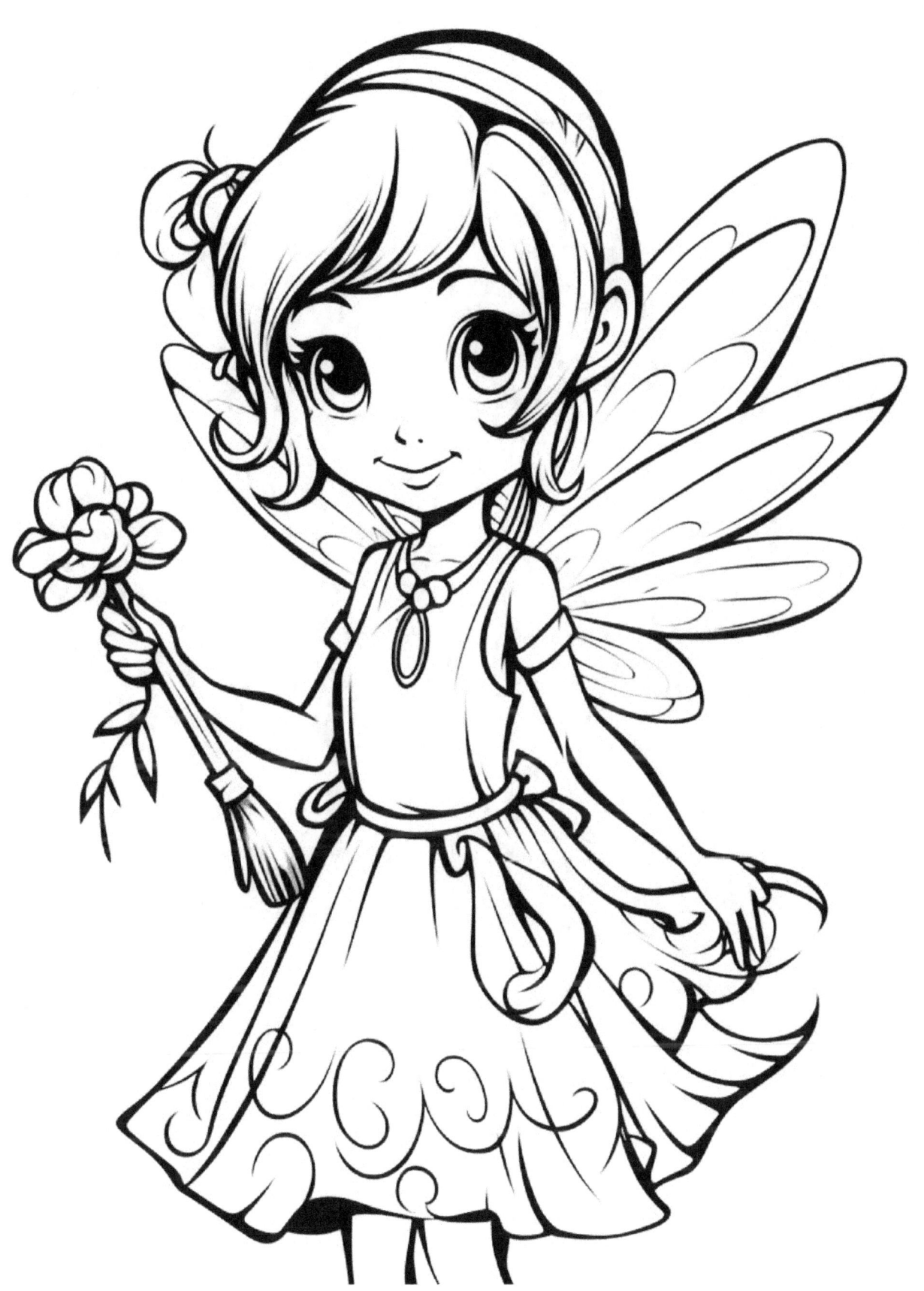

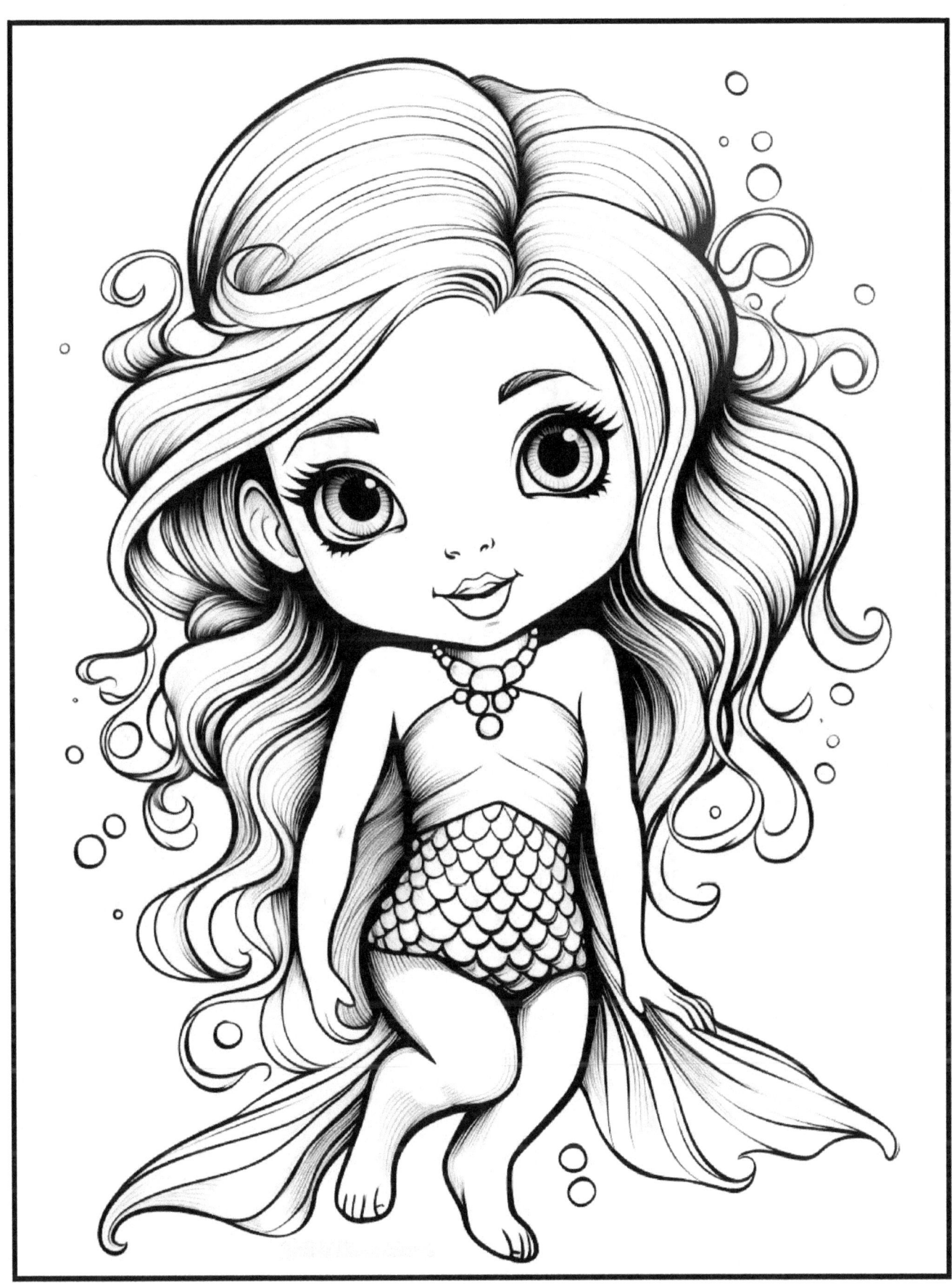

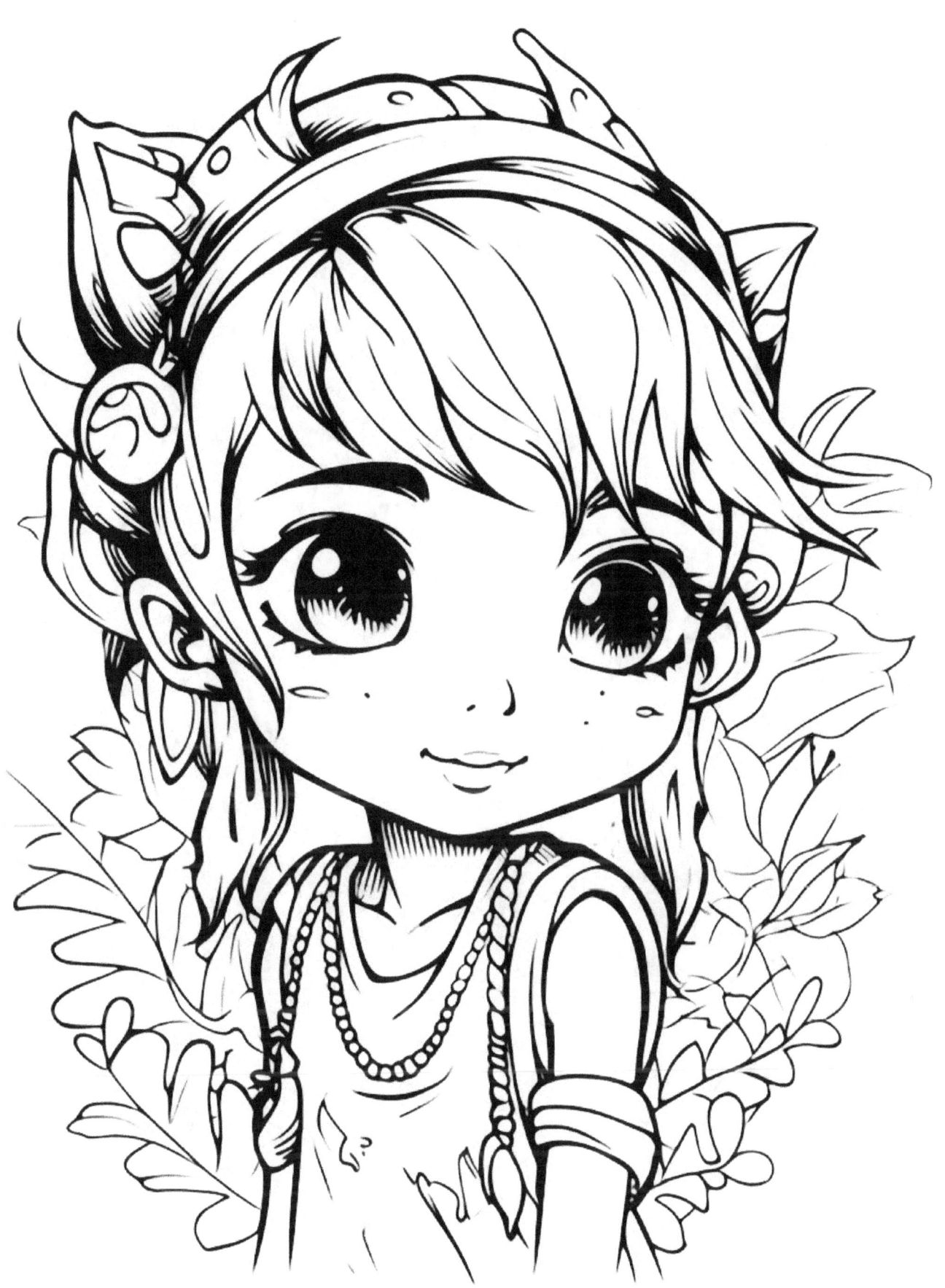

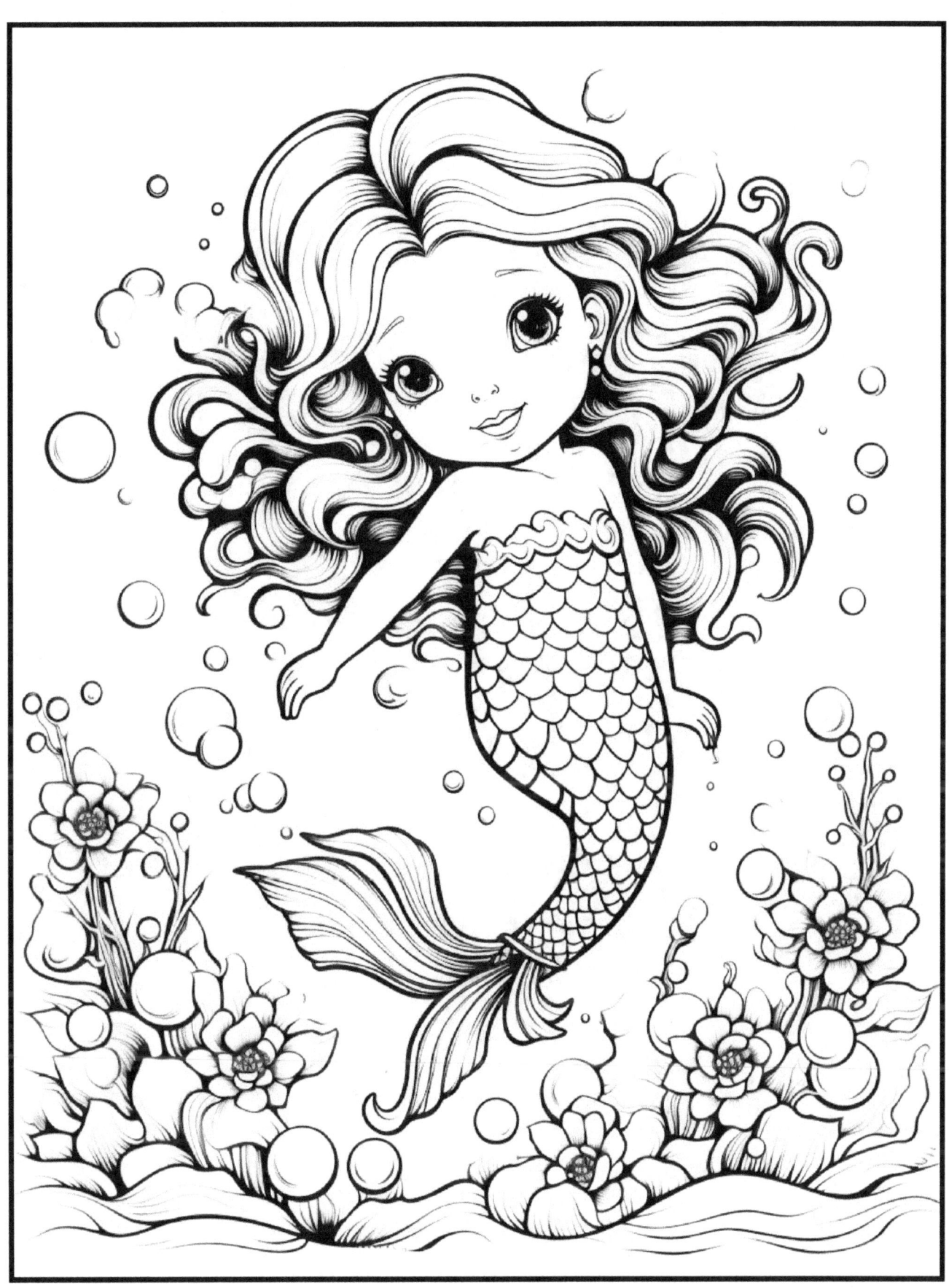

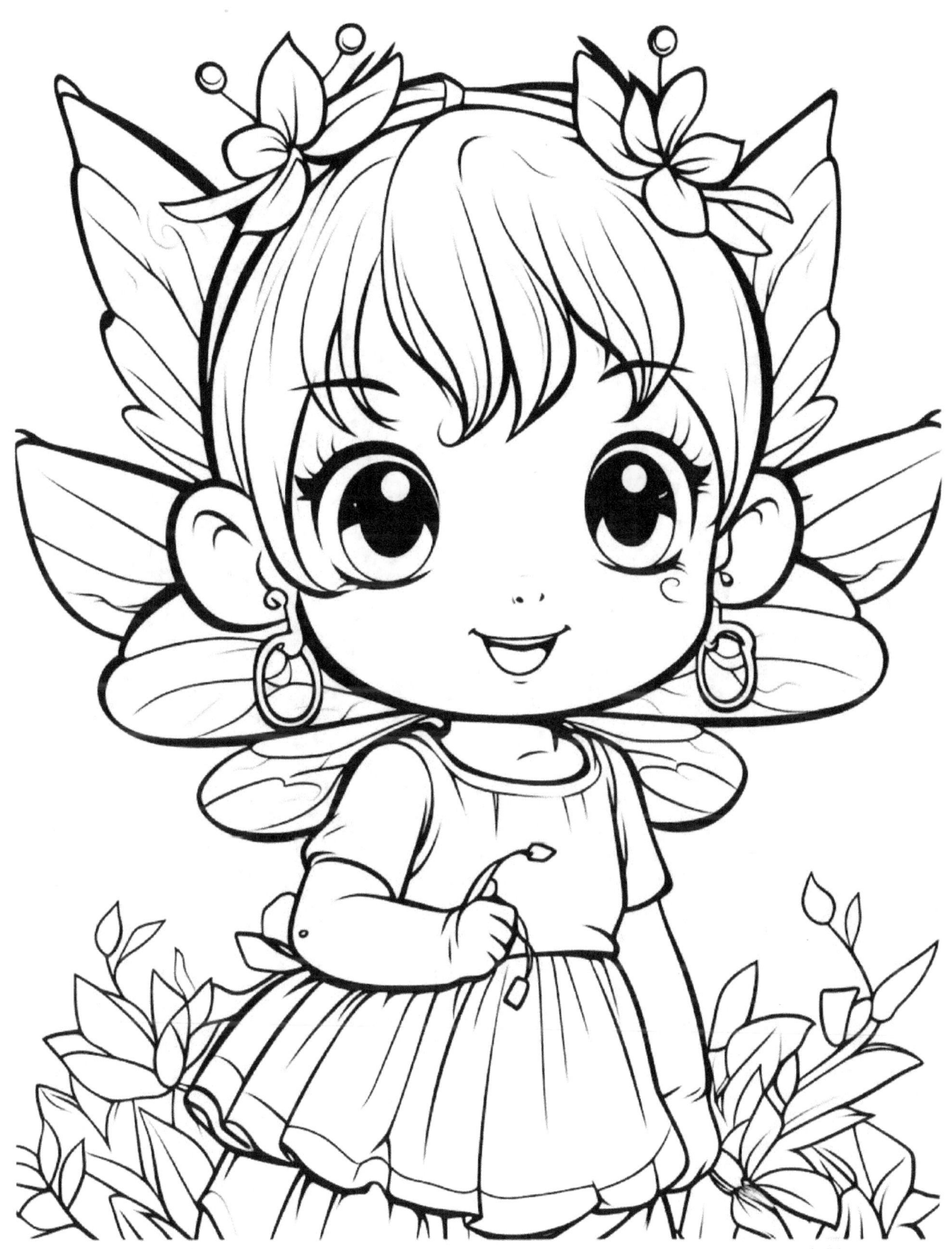

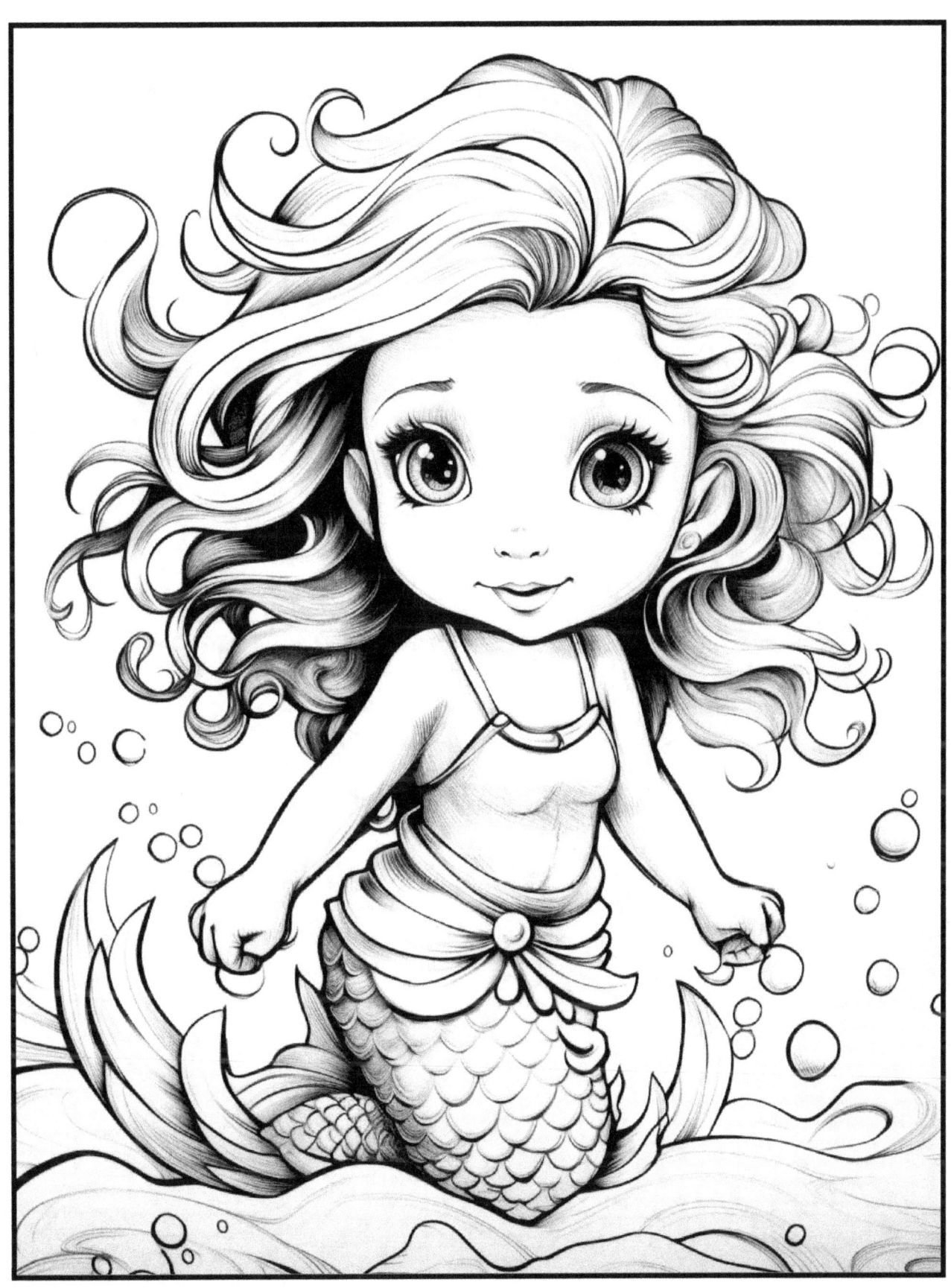

Thank You So Much For Spending Some Time Being Creative With Us.

Please take a look at some of our other activity and coloring books. As well as our large collection of journals.

AH64Designs

www.ingramcontent.com/pod-product-compliance
Lightning Source LLC
Chambersburg PA
CBHW082222220526
45470CB00010B/3278